W9-BNJ-777

The Gift of CHRISTMAS

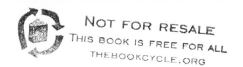

NOT FOR RESALE
THIS BOOK IS FREE FOR ALL
THEBOOKCYCLE.ORG

The Gift of
CHRISTMAS

Compiled by
JAYNE BOWMAN

Illustrated by
PETER CHURCH

The C. R. Gibson Company, Norwalk, Connecticut

Copyright © MCMLXXXVII by
The C. R. Gibson Company
Published by the C. R. Gibson Company
Norwalk, Connecticut 06856
All rights reserved
Printed in the United States of America
ISBN 0-8378-1822-2
The acknowledgments that appear on
pages 90–91 hereby constitute an
extension of this copyright page.

CONTENTS

O Holy Night

Love…The Perfect Gift

Keeping Christmas

Therefore the Lord himself shall give you a sign; Behold, a virgin shall conceive, and bear a son, and shall call his name Immanuel.

For unto us a child is born, unto us a son is given: and the government shall be upon his shoulder: and his name shall be called Wonderful, Counsellor, The mighty God, The everlasting Father, The Prince of Peace.

Isaiah 7:14; 9:6

And so it was, that, while they were there, the days were accomplished that she should be delivered. And she brought forth her firstborn son, and wrapped him in swaddling clothes, and laid him in a manger; because there was no room for them in the inn.

Luke 2:6–7

CHRISTMAS DAYBREAK

Before the paling of the stars,
Before the winter morn,
Before the earliest cockcrow,
Jesus Christ was born:
Born in a stable,
Cradled in a manger,
In the world His hands had made,
Born a stranger.

Priest and king lay fast asleep
In Jerusalem,
Young and old lay fast asleep
In crowded Bethlehem:
Saint and angel, ox and ass,
Kept a watch together,
Before the Christmas daybreak
In the winter weather.

Jesus on His Mother's breast
In the stable cold,
Spotless Lamb of God was He,
Shepherd of the fold.
Let us kneel with Mary Maid,
With Joseph bent and hoary,
With saint and angel, ox and ass,
To hail the King of Glory.

Christina Georgina Rossetti

THE CHRISTMAS CHILD

The Truth was far too great and vast for human minds to see—
and so God made it simple, something small enough to be—
held within a woman's arms, a tiny helpless mite—cradled in
a little manger on a winter's night....If life's meaning you would
seek, it's here for you to find—in the Holy Child of Christmas,
Saviour of mankind.

Patience Strong

O HOLY NIGHT

O holy night! The stars are brightly shining,
It is the night of the dear Savior's birth;
Long lay the world in sin and error pining,
Till He appeared and the soul felt its worth.
A thrill of hope the weary world rejoices,
For yonder breaks a new and glorious morn.

Fall on your knees
Oh, hear the angel voices!
O night divine
O night when Christ was born!
O night
O holy night, O night divine!

Help us rightly to remember the birth of Jesus, that we may share in the song of the angels, the gladness of the shepherds, and the worship of the Wise Men.

Robert Louis Stevenson

THE MAID-SERVANT AT THE INN

"It's queer," she said, "I see the light
    As plain as I beheld it then,
All silver-like and calm and bright—
    We've not had stars like that again!

"And she was such a gentle thing
    To birth a baby in the cold.
The barn was dark and frightening—
    This new one's better than the old.

"I mind my eyes were full of tears,
    For I was young, and quick distressed,
But she was less than me in years
    That held a son against her breast.

"I never saw a sweeter child—
    The little one, the darling one!—
I mind I told her, when he smiled
    You'd know he was his mother's son.

"It's queer that I should see them so—
    The time they came to Bethlehem
Was more than thirty years ago;
    I've prayed that all is well with them."

Dorothy Parker

17

HIS MONOGRAM

The very ordinariness of that first Christmas pleads knowingly and persuasively to common people. Christmas came to little Bethlehem that we might know that no place is unknown to God; at the stroke of twelve to remind us that there is no moment of the day or night when He is absent from us; to young Mary to convince us that all life is dear to Him; and in a Child that we may sense that all life is in His hands. Christmas is His monogram, stenciled on our hearts, recalling to us year by year that "no more is God a Stranger."

When Christmas Came To Bethlehem

Love came down at Christmas,
Love all lovely, Love Divine;
Love was born at Christmas,
Star and Angels gave the sign.

Christina Georgina Rossetti

Dear Lord, I offer Thee this day
All I shall think, or do, or say.

Author Unknown

MESSAGE OF CHRISTMAS

Welcome Christmas once again! Come blizzard, snow or rime—it cannot dim the joy that fills our hearts at this glad time. The days are brief, the nights are long, the skies are bleak and drear—but a glory shines about the ending of the year. The glory of a wondrous thing: the Christmas mystery. The strange and lovely story of our Lord's nativity. The only hope that's left to man upon this troubled earth—the hope God gave at Bethlehem at the Messiah's birth…Welcome sweet and holy day, the day of Christ the King. Once again the world awaits the message that you bring.

Patience Strong

CONTINUING ADVENTURE

As we leave Bethlehem, we ought to leave behind old grudges, old fears, old sorrows. We ought to continue our adventure of life by praising God and by walking on new and better roads. Sometime during the winter we shall need the friendly spirit of Christmas. Sometime in the spring we shall want the hope of Christmas. Let us not pack up the true spirit of Christmas when we put away the decorations.

Christmas In Our Hearts

A CHRISTMAS SONG

Everywhere, everywhere, Christmas to-night!
Christmas in lands of fir tree and pine;
Christmas in lands of palm tree and vine;
Christmas where snow peaks stand solemn and white;
Christmas where cornfields lie sunny and bright:
Everywhere, everywhere, Christmas to-night!

Phillips Brooks

LOVE
The Perfect Gift

If, instead of a gem or even a flower, we could cast the gift of a lovely thought into the heart of a friend, that would be giving as angels give.

George MacDonald

THE TOUCH OF A HAND

Our church was celebrating Christmas Eve with a children's program. Its chapel had special memories for me. Only eight months previously, the memorial service for my husband of 44 years had been held there.

On my own now, I settled into a seat near the aisle. During the opening prayer I noticed a young girl, about ten years old, standing in the aisle, looking for a place to sit. Motioning to her to come in, I turned my knees and the girl slid past and sat down. The beautiful program continued, with the children participating in songs, poems and recitals. The climax was the singing of "Silent Night." As the children's voices cho_used this most beautiful of Christmas hymns, memories of past Christmases with my husband flooded back. My eyes filled with tears and I held a handkerchief to my mouth, trying to control myself. Then I felt my neighbor's small hand creep into my lap. She took my hand and gave it a comforting squeeze. My heart swelled with sudden joy.

As I look back on that evening, I give thanks for this simplest and loveliest of Christmas gifts—the touch of a hand.

Mary Janes

Silent night, holy night,
All is calm, all is bright
Round yon Virgin Mother and Child.
Holy Infant, so tender and mild,
Sleep in heavenly peace,
Sleep in heavenly peace.

CHRISTMAS DAY IN THE MORNING

He waked suddenly and completely. It was four o'clock, the hour at which his father had always called him to get up and help with the milking. Strange how the habits of his youth clung to him still! Fifty years ago, and his father had been dead for thirty years, and yet he waked at four o'clock in the morning. He had trained himself to turn over and go to sleep, but this morning, because it was Christmas, he did not try to sleep.

He slipped back in time, as he did so easily nowadays. He was fifteen years old and still on his father's farm. He loved his father. He had not known it until one day a few days before Christmas, when he overheard what his father was saying to his mother.

"Mary, I hate to call Rob in the mornings. He's growing so fast, and he needs his sleep. If you could see how he sleeps when I go in to wake him up! I wish I could manage alone."

"Well, you can't, Adam." His mother's voice was brisk. "Besides, he isn't a child anymore. It's time he took his turn."

"Yes," his father said slowly. "But I sure do hate to wake him."

When he heard these words, something in him woke: his father loved him! He had never thought of it before, taking for granted the tie of their blood. Neither his father nor his mother talked about loving their children—they had no time for such things. There was always so much to do on a farm.

Now that he knew his father loved him, there would be no more loitering in the mornings and having to be called again.

27

He got up after that, stumbling with sleep, and pulled on his clothes, his eyes tight shut, but he got up.

And then on the night before Christmas, that year when he was fifteen, he lay for a few minutes thinking about the next day. They were poor, and most of the excitement was in the turkey they had raised themselves and in the mince pies his mother made. His sisters sewed presents and his mother and father always bought something he needed, not only a warm jacket, maybe, but something more, such as a book. And he saved and bought them each something, too.

He wished, that Christmas he was fifteen, he had a better present for his father. As usual, he had gone to the ten-cent store and bought a tie. It had seemed nice enough until he lay thinking the night before Christmas, and then he wished that he had heard his father and mother talking in time for him to save for something better.

He lay on his side, his head supported by his elbow, and looked out of his attic window. The stars were bright, much brighter than he ever remembered seeing them, and one was so bright he wondered if it were really the star of Bethlehem.

"Dad," he had once asked when he was a little boy, "what is a stable?"

"It's just a barn," his father had replied, "like ours."

Then Jesus had been born in a barn, and to a barn the shepherds and the Wise Men had come, bringing their Christmas gifts!

The thought stuck him like a silver dagger. Why should he not give his father a special gift, too, out there in the barn? He could get up early, earlier than four o'clock, and he could creep into the barn and get all the milking done. He'd do it alone, milk and clean up, and then when his father went in to start the milking, he'd see it all done. And he would know who had done it.

At a quarter to three, he got up and put on his clothes. He crept downstairs, careful of the creaky boards, and let himself out. The big star hung lower over the barn roof, a reddish gold. The cows looked at him, sleepy and surprised.

"So, boss," he whispered. They accepted him placidly, and he fetched some hay for each cow and then got the milking pail and the big milk cans.

He had never milked all alone before, but it seemed almost easy. He kept thinking about his father's surprise. His father would come in and call him, saying that he would get things started while Rob was getting dressed. He'd go to the barn, open the door, and then he'd go to get the two big empty milk cans. But they wouldn't be waiting or empty; they'd be standing in the milk house, filled.

The task went more easily then he had ever known it to before. Milking for once was not a chore. It was something else, a gift to his father who loved him. He finished, the two milk cans were full, and he covered them and closed the milk-house door carefully, making sure of the latch. He put the stool in its place by the door and hung up the clean milk pail. Then he went out of the barn and barred the door behind him.

Back in his room, he had only a minute to pull off his clothes in the darkness and jump into bed, for he heard his father up. He put the covers over his head to silence his quick breathing.

The door opened.

"Rob!" his father called. "We have to get up, son, even if it is Christmas."

"Aw-right," he said sleepily.

"I'll go on out," his father said. "I'll get things started."

The door closed and he lay still, laughing to himself. In just a few minutes his father would know. His dancing heart was ready to jump from his body.

The minutes were endless—ten, fifteen, he did not know how many—and he heard his father's footsteps again. The door opened and he lay still.

"Rob!"

"Yes, Dad—"

His father was laughing, a queer sobbing sort of a laugh. "Thought you'd fool me, did you?" His father was standing beside his bed, feeling for him, pulling away the cover.

"It's for Christmas, Dad!"

He found his father and clutched him in a great hug. He felt his father's arms go around him. It was dark, and they could not see each other's faces.

"Son, I thank you. Nobody ever did a nicer thing—"

"Oh, Dad, I want you to know—I do want to be good!" The words broke from him of their own will. He did not know what to say. His heart was bursting with love.

"Well, I reckon I can go back to bed and sleep," his father said after a moment. "No, hark—the little ones are waked up. Come to think of it, son, I've never seen you children when you first saw the Christmas tree. I was always in the barn. Come on!"

He got up and pulled on his clothes again, and they went down to the Christmas tree; and soon the sun was creeping up to where the star had been. Oh, what a Christmas, and how his heart had nearly burst again with shyness and pride as his father told his mother and made the younger children listen about how he, Rob, had got up all by himself.

"The best Christmas gift I ever had, and I'll remember it, son, every year on Christmas morning, so long as I live."

They had both remembered it, and now that his father was dead he remembered it alone: that blessed Christmas dawn when, alone with the cows in the barn, he had made his first gift of true love.

Pearl S. Buck

STORY OF LOVE

Bethlehem surely means many things to many people, and no genuine meaning is without significance. But towering over all, Christmas is a story of divine and human love. Christmas is a festival of love which has a magnetlike tug on our hearts. A compelling, compassionate, and all-encompassing love explains the attractiveness of this day. Without love, there could never have been a first Christmas. Apart from the love we bring and the love we offer and receive, Christmas would be as dreary as an all-day drizzle.

When Christmas Came To Bethlehem

It is the fatherly feelings in a child
and the childlike feelings in a father
that reach out to each other eternal
hands of love.

George MacDonald

HEAVENLY CHILD

The tiny parking lot behind the Happy Hours Kindergarten was already filled but they found a space across the street. Even from there, they could hear the children singing carols loudly.

"Well, it's noisier than it was in September," Molly said, trying to laugh. "Remember how sort of strained it was then, meeting all those parents and children for the first time? And Kim so quiet...."

"She sure wasn't quiet tonight," Louis said, as they got out of the car. "The whole time I was driving her over she never stopped chattering about the picture she's going to show us and the fact that she got picked to come early to help mix the punch. She's made a great adjustment, honey. Don't forget, these are the first children she's really had a chance to know."

"And the first complete families," Molly added, "ones she could relate to." Their own friends were mostly the parents of teen-agers. She and Lou had waited a long time before they accepted the fact that there would be no child of their own, longer still before they had seriously considered adoption.

When they had finally made the decision, however, they had been in complete accord about the next step. Their parents and friends had been startled. Even now, five years later, Molly could recall her mother's concern: "But *why* a Vietnamese baby? Surely you can qualify for a child from a local agency, one of your own race...."

"Children like that are more easily placed," Molly had explained. "Lou and I want to share our lives with a child who needs us, a child who wouldn't have a home if we didn't take him."

"You're asking for problems," her mother had said worriedly. "Granted, there is nothing cuter than an Oriental baby, but when he gets older and compares his family to others, will he ever really feel he belongs?"

"Of course," Molly had cried, thrusting the warning from her.

But had she, she now wondered, disposed of it too quickly? Would it come back to haunt her on this peaceful night of the children's party?

Kim had defied them right from the start by not being "a cute Oriental baby." The child who was carried out to them at the airport was pathetic. Dull eyes stared lifelessly out from under a tangle of dirty hair; a distended belly bulged beneath a cheap cotton dress. Matchstick arms hung limply.

When Molly had reached out, Kim had begun to cry.

"She's frightened," the woman from the agency had said. "She's had a hard time. You'll win her over. Just feed her and love her."

"We will," Molly had promised.

And they had fed her and loved her. Oh, how they had loved her! And how wonderful it had been to watch her become a truly heavenly child, robust and happy.

Kim was over two years old when she finally began to walk and, at about the same time, she began to speak. Her first words were "Mama" and Dada," to her parents' delight, and Molly's mother, whose heart had been won completely, had started a campaign to teach her to say "Nana."

By the time she was four, Kim had become a definite personality, funny, endearing and stubborn. She had also developed a strong feeling about her own identity.

"I am Kim Jordan," she would say in a tone that invited no argument. "My daddy is Louis Jordan. My mommy is Molly Jordan. My grandma is Nana Jordan."

"No. Grandma is Nana Elliot," Molly would correct her. "She has a different name from ours."

But Kim would not accept this. "No," she would state firmly. "We are all in one family, all the same."

"I guess it's time we went into the adoption story with her," Lou said when he heard this.

So that night they had sat on Kim's bed and told her about their loneliness before she came to them, and about how they had sent away to a far country....

"What was I doing there?" Kim asked. "In that funny place all by myself?"

"You were born there," Louis began.

Kim interrupted. "That's a dumb story. Tell something good."

So Louis had told *Goldilocks* and listening, Molly had become fully conscious for the first time how much little brown bears looked like big brown bears, and how vulnerable her child was.

She musn't be hurt, Molly had thought fiercely. She mustn't ever be hurt.

And at the same time the question had risen unbidden within her: Did we do the right thing? Will she thank us later? Or will the time come when she looks at us and sees us not as parents but as members of an alien race with white skin and round eyes?

The thought had come even stronger when it was time to start Kim in kindergarten. It was Louis who brought up Happy Hours.

"It's got a good reputation," he said. "It's fully integrated, with a little of everything. A Japanese guy at work sends his boy there."

"These other kids," Molly had asked, "are they...from mixed families like ours?"

"Who knows?" Louis had said. "They're having an open house next Thursday. We can go and find out what it's all about."

So they had enrolled Kim. Molly had known in her heart that this was best. They had attended the open house and the families had been there—white, black, red, and golden-skinned families—but each consistent within itself.

Kim had clung to Molly's hand. She had stared about her silently through widened eyes, and Molly had thought: She sees. She is beginning to realize. It will not be long.

That had been in the fall. As the next months passed, Kim's initial shyness vanished. She liked her teachers. She liked painting. She liked music and games and making letters.

"But she seems different," Molly remarked to Louis. "We're not as close. It's as though she's turning outward, toward other people, away from us."

"Isn't that natural?" Louis had answered. "After all, she's not a baby. It's time she became more independent. Don't worry so, honey. Kim loves us; she knows we love her."

And now he said the same thing.

As they crossed the snowy lawn the noise grew louder, and when they went in it poured upon them in a wave of festivity. The big front room was ablaze with color; paper streamers of

red and green draped the ceiling, and a tall tree glowed with rainbow lights. In the center a long table held platters of cookies and a shimmering punch bowl.

People were everywhere—mothers, fathers, grandparents—but the kindergartners themselves were the stars. They rushed about, chirping like happy sparrows, as they dragged adults by the hand, pointing out paintings and projects, giggling and squealing and bubbling with joy.

Kim was standing motionless beside the punch bowl. When she saw Louis and Molly her face came to life. Handing the ladle to the girl beside her, she worked her way toward them. "Did you see my picture?" she asked.

"Not yet," Molly said. "Where is it?"

"There on the wall," Kim said.

Turning, Molly saw that the far wall was covered with children's drawings. Two dozen proud Josephs guarded two dozen gentle Marys, and two dozen mangers tilted precariously in as many directions. Angels perched daringly on rooftops, and a varied assortment of lopsided stars gleamed on high.

"Which is yours?" Molly asked, and even as she spoke she felt her husband's arm go around her. His other hand dropped to rest on his daughter's glossy black head.

Then she saw it—the picture of the blond Joseph bent protectively over his blond Mary. From the manger, on a mound of hay so high that any less perfect babe would have rolled off onto the stable floor, a raven-haired, almond-eyed Baby beamed contentedly up at His parents.

Lois Duncan

CRADLE HYMN

Away in a manger, no crib for a bed,
The little Lord Jesus laid down His
   sweet head.
The stars in the bright sky looked down
   where He lay—
The little Lord Jesus, asleep on the hay.

Martin Luther

A YOUNG GIRL'S GIFT

As I prepared breakfast, the week-before-Christmas tread-mill whirled round and round in my head: must do this, must do that…

Only when the eggs and coffee were ready did I realize that my daughter Andrea was still standing by the window in her blue robe, dreamily twisting one long strand of dark-honey hair between her fingers.

"Anything wrong?" I asked.

She jumped a little, as though my voice had recalled her from a dream. "I was just wondering what to wear for the Christmas concert. I can't decide between my red wool and the green taffeta."

Andrea plays the flute in the school orchestra. "Either dress should be fine," I said, wishing she would eat so we could clear the table.

She sat and began to pick at her food slowly. My nerves tight-ened: had to wrap packages, get to the post office. Masses of silvery paper and bright ribbon awaited me, tags saying From and To, and a red crayon for writing Do Not Open Until Christmas.

When the last package was ready for mailing, I ran upstairs to get my coat. Passing Andrea's room, I stopped in surprise. Although she was no paragon of neatness, it was a long time since she had left her room in such a mess. Her bed was unmade, her bureau cluttered, her closet door ajar. I glanced

in, then turned away as I saw a few unwrapped presents on the shelf. But even that quick glance was enough to see that only a fraction of her shopping was accomplished. And where in the world was she now?

I sent Brad to find her. In a minute she appeared, carrying her flute. "I—I was just practicing in the garage," she stammered. She looked around the room vaguely. "Gosh, it needs straightening, doesn't it?" "That was my feeling," I replied grimly. "And, if I may venture a guess, a few presents need to be bought." My feckless child grinned. "Are you hinting for a gift, Mom?" In a ludicrously haughty social voice, she assured me, "You

shall not be forgotten, never fear. Night and day I am planning, planning, abrim with yuletide spirit."

As the week progressed, I felt increasingly tired and rushed. The hours began to speed up, like an old movie film. Newspaper ads tolled the countdown: six more, five more, four more shopping days. It was impossible, absolutely out of the question, that I would ever get the last gift bought, the last tag written, the last special meal cooked.

Russ's sense of doom equaled mine. Work was extra heavy at his office. Even Brad began to look harried as he scampered through multitudinous festivities at school and Scouts. Of us all, only Andrea remained buoyant—and small wonder, I thought, since responsibility sat on her so lightly.

I was puzzled, though, by an odd remoteness about her, and she seemed evasive when I questioned why she came home late from school or left unusually early in the morning. Once I heard her whispering on the phone in a voice of suppressed excitement, and caught the words, "No, not an inkling, I'm sure of it."

On one of those last mornings, I decorated and baked Christmas cookies. There were several interruptions, and I slipped farther and farther behind schedule. At noon, with guests coming for lunch, I set about tidying the kitchen. I opened the dishwasher—but it was full already, and not of clean dishes. Andrea had loaded the machine after breakfast and failed to start it.

Tears filled my eyes. Suddenly it all seemed too much: the dirty dishes, the too-tight schedule, Andrea's negligence. Above all, Christmas was just too much. It didn't seem worth it.

Depressed and furious, I dumped my mixing bowls into the sink and fixed lunch. When my guests left, I had barely time enough to do all the dishes before picking up Andrea at school to drive her to her flute lesson.

I pulled up at the high school at three o'clock, still seething. Andrea's coltish, long-haired figure detached itself from a group of friends and ran toward me. I almost weakened at the sight of the funny, half-skipping run, left over from her bouncy little-girlhood. She tumbled happily into the car, bubbling with some bit of high-school news. But as she saw my face, her gaiety gave way to sudden apprehension.

"What's wrong?"

I told her. She couldn't remember anything, she was untidy, inconsiderate. "I don't know what you're thinking of, you go dreaming along..." We had nearly reached the music school before I ran out of things to say. Beside me, Andrea sat perfectly quiet. I did not glance at her, but I could imagine the set of that clear young profile; the fixed expression of the wide hazel eyes. When I stopped the car, she got out and walked wordlessly away.

Suddenly I felt sad and ashamed. Did Christmas have to be like this? Responsible for the "success" of the day, I was churning over every detail, trying to make sure nothing was forgotten. Yet something was missing: the dazzling light of a Star in the East, the birth of a miraculous Child...the promise and the wonder had escaped me.

That evening, we rushed through our dinner. It was the night of the high-school Christmas concert. Along with other families, Russ and Brad and I took our seats in the auditorium.

I saw Andrea, in her green taffeta, sit down at her music stand in the pit. Up on the stage, the boys and girls of the chorus massed in a double line. Russ and I smiled; it was the warm, familiar moment of assessment: how tall Johnny Evans was getting, how pretty Susie looked, Caroline Miller had cut her hair....

As the concert started, my tension began to drain away. I listened, relaxed and moved by the special atmosphere that these young people created. Old and new songs about snow and reindeer alternated with reverent Christmas music. Between pieces, we all exchanged contented glances with our neighbors.

At last the music teacher announced the final selection:

"Jesu, Joy of Man's Desiring." He added, "For the last number we have a soloist. Because she wanted it to be a surprise for her family, her name is not listed on the program." Smiling, he looked down into the orchestra pit: "Andrea Hill."

I gasped. My tears blurred her image as Andrea rose and, to the applause of that packed auditorium, took her place on the stage in front of the massed chorus. Just before she raised the flute to her lips, she looked straight at her father and brother and me, and gave us a wide, joyful smile.

I smiled back, tremulous. Russ tucked a handkerchief into my hand. With one accord, we turned to Brad just as he turned to us. Our unity with each other and with the radiant girl on the stage seemed to encircle the four of us, out of all the world.

Did the music sound so beautiful because our child's instrument led it? I don't think so. All the fresh young voices were beautiful, and all the hopeful, shining faces.

But most beautiful of all was the sense of wonder that filled me. I remembered the practicing, out of hearing, in the garage;

the extra time spent at school; the details ignored, the little things undone—while she did this big thing. Instinctively wise, Andrea had grasped a truth that had eluded me: that dutifulness is less than love.

With her love, she had presented me, now and forever, with the music and the meaning of Christmas. That was Andrea's gift.

Elizabeth Starr Hill

GIFTS ON MY ALTAR

Place these gifts on my altar this Christmas;
Gifts that are mine, as the years are mine:
The quiet hopes that flood the earnest cargo
of my dreams:
The best of all good things for those I love,
A fresh new trust for all whose faith is dim.
The love of life, God's precious gift in reach of all:
Seeing in each day the seeds of the morrow,
Finding in each struggle the strength of renewal,
Seeking in each person the face of my brother.
I place these gifts on my altar this Christmas;
Gifts that are mine, as the years are mine.

Howard Thurman

SNEAD'S CHRISTMAS GIFT

Snead, a great, dark, gentle, giant of a man, did a bit of gardening and odd jobs on the suburban street where I spent my early childhood. He was a person to whom young boys instinctively reached out—patient, kind, with uncanny understanding. Snead knew all about you just by looking at you. When Snead would walk through our neighborhood, there would be a chorus of "Snead, Snead!" in his wake. Boys would bring him snakes, show off a new baseball glove, ask him how to fix a bike. But mostly we just wanted to be near him—his calm, kind presence.

The best thing that could possibly happen to a boy on Muriel Road was to get a ride with Snead in his car. It was an ancient Wills St. Clair, four-door sedan with the back seat removed to contain a marvelous jumble of tools, gardening implements, spare parts, tire chains, inner tubes, and Snead's violin.

Once, with about five of us aboard, the stately sedan had a flat tire. It was paradise. The flat meant: a) we could get dirty; b) we could rummage in the Wills St. Clair's interior for tools and parts; and c) we got to spend an extra half-hour watching Snead, a wizard mechanic, at work.

One golden day in December I wangled a ride to town in the Wills St. Clair—just Snead and I. As we rumbled along, I asked, "Do you think we might have a flat tire, Snead?"

"It's entirely possible," Snead said, "but I certainly hope not."

"Remember last summer when we had the flat tire?" I asked. "Wasn't that fun?"

"Well, I really didn't see the glory in it," Snead said.

"Snead," I said, "would it make you angry if I prayed we had a flat tire today?"

Snead reached over and gave my ear a little tug. "No, except that we're going to put God in a fix, praying at cross purposes."

"If you don't mind, then, Snead, I'm going to put a flat tire on my Christmas wish list, since it's only two weeks away." I closed my eyes and mumbled a little prayer.

When I looked up and over at Snead, he looked thoughtful.

Once in town, Snead pulled into a lot behind the hardware store. "Run in and get me a five-pound bag of rock salt and a box of twenty-amp fuses," Snead said, handing me a dollar. "Remember now, twenty-amp."

Returning five minutes later I found Snead, his floppy felt hat pulled over his eyes, asleep. I plopped the hardware sack down between us and with a solid thunk pulled the heavy car door shut. And the minute I sat down, I knew my foolish little prayer had been answered. The stately sedan had a definite rearward tilt.

"Snead," I cried out, "we've got a flat tire!"

"Well, well," Snead said, pushing his hat back on his head, "so we do."

Snead and I went through the entire fascinating flat tire ritual again—with me fetching the jack, tire irons and spare inner tube. He let me help stuff the tube in the tire and lower the jack once he'd got the tire back on. The only difference between the other flat tire and this one was that Snead never grumbled once.

Taking this to mean that he had warmed to the project, I

asked, "See, Snead, it *is* fun to change a tire, right?"

Snead gave my ear another little tug and said, "Well, son, it is when you're along."

I said, "It's not even Christmas, and my best wish has already come true!"

Well, it's been nearly forty years since Snead and I had our flat tire together, but I remember it whenever there's an especially nice sunny day along about Christmastime. It was my first, and my best, lesson in giving. Perhaps you'd understand what I mean if you'd overheard Snead telling my mother, "Sorry to get the boy home late, but I had to arrange a little flat tire for him downtown."

James McDermott

JIMMY AND HIS COWBOY BELT

Two or three days before Christmas last year, a group of children who come often to our house for stories on Monday afternoons came and we sat in a small room around a little Franklin stove in which a welcome fire was burning. We sat there and we talked about Christmas. I was aware that there was a shine from the firelight in the eyes of those boys and girls and on their wind-polished cheeks.

But no shine equalled that which gleamed from the buckle on the cowboy belt that Jimmy was wearing. Nine-year-old Jimmy was something of a swaggerer, but he liked books and liked to

come and listen to stories. I had known for a long time that his cowboy belt was a prized possession, and the buckle was something marvelous.

We talked about Christmas for a little while. And then I read them one of the loveliest stories I know—Rachel Field's "All Through The Night"—a simple retelling of the Christmas story. There was a great silence while I read—the only sounds the words of the ageless tale and the crackling of the fire in the stove.

When the story was over, no one spoke for a moment. I knew that it could not be a long moment, because something like that can't be held very long—with fifteen or twenty children for whom the deliciousness of Christmas is only two days away.

I was the first one, however, to break the spell with words other than the story. I said, "What if we put on our coats and hats and went out of this little house and across the field in the snow and, dark as it is, went down the slope, across the brook, and into the woods? What if there we came upon the stable and the manger and the Baby? What could we give to him?"

Again there was a moment of utter silence. Then Jimmy put his hand on his middle and said, "I'd give him my cowboy belt."

Elizabeth Yates

What can I give him,
Poor as I am?
If I were a shepherd
I would bring a lamb;
If I were a wise man
I would do my part;
Yet what I can I give him—
Give my heart.

Christina Georgina Rossetti

DRAMA AT GATE 67

The surge of holiday traffic would have taxed the congested
Atlanta airport under the best of circumstances. But, as Christmas neared, nature had added an ice storm that stranded
thousands of travelers.

As the midnight hour tolled, weary pilgrims clustered around
ticket counters, conferring anxiously with agents whose cheer-
iness had long since evaporated; they, too, longed to be home.
Others gathered at the newsstands to thumb silently through
paperback books. A few managed to doze, contorted into
human pretzels, in uncomfortable seats.

If there was a common bond among this diverse throng, it
was loneliness—pervasive, inescapable, suffocating loneliness. But airport decorum required that each traveler maintain
his invisible barrier against all the others. Better to be lonely
than to be involved, which inevitably meant listening to complaints, and heaven knows everyone had enough complaints
of his own already.

Just beneath the surface, in fact, lurked a competitive hostility. After all, there were more passengers than seats; when an occasional plane managed to break out, more travelers stayed behind than made it aboard. "Standby," "Reservation Confirmed," "First Class Passenger" were words that settled priorities and bespoke money, power, influence, foresight—or the lack thereof.

Gate 67 was a microcosm of the whole cavernous airport. Scarcely more than a glassed-in cubicle, it was jammed with travelers hoping to fly to New Orleans, Dallas and points west.

Except for the fortunate few traveling in pairs, there was little conversation. A salesman stared absently into space, as if resigned. A young mother cradled an infant to her breast, gently rocking in a vain effort to soothe the soft whimpering.

And there was a man in a finely tailored suit who somehow seemed impervious to the collective suffering. There was a certain indifference about his manner. He was absorbed in some arcane paper work. Figuring the year-end corporate profits, perhaps. A nerve-frayed traveler sitting nearby, observing this busy man, might have indulged in a cynical fantasy: "His clothes are different, but he can't disguise his nature. It's Ebenezer Scrooge."

Suddenly, the sullen silence was broken by a commotion. A young man in uniform, no more than 19 years old, was in animated conversation with the desk agent. The boy held a low-priority ticket. But he must, he pleaded, get to New Orleans, so that he could take the bus on to the obscure Louisiana village he called home.

The agent wearily told him the prospects were poor for the next 24 hours, maybe longer.

The boy grew frantic. He was soon to be sent to Vietnam. If he did not make this flight, he might never again spend Christmas at home.

Even the businessman looked up from his cryptic computations to show a guarded interest. The agent clearly was moved, even a bit embarrassed. But he could offer only sympathy, not hope. The boy hovered about the departure desk, casting wild and anxious looks around the crowded room, as if seeking but one friendly face.

Finally, the agent hoarsely announced that the flight was ready for boarding. The pilgrims heaved themselves up, gathered their belongings, and shuffled down the small corridor to the waiting craft. Twenty, 30, 100—until there were no more seats. The agent turned to the frantic young man and shrugged.

Inexplicably, the businessman had lingered behind. Now he stepped forward. "I have a confirmed ticket," he quietly told the agent. "I'd like to give my seat to this young man."

The agent stared incredulously; then he motioned to the soldier. Unable to speak, tears streaming down his face, the boy in olive drab shook hands with the man in gray flannel, who simply murmured, "Good luck. Have a fine Christmas. Good luck."

As the plane door closed and the engines began their rising whine, the businessman turned away, clutching his briefcase, and trudged toward the all-night coffee bar.

No more than a few among the thousands stranded there at the Atlanta airport witnessed the drama at Gate 67. But for these, the sullenness, the frustration, the hostility, all dissolved into a glow.

The lights of the departing plane blinked, starlike, as the craft moved off into the darkness. The infant slept silently now on the breast of the young mother. Perhaps another flight would be leaving before many more hours; but those who saw were less impatient. The glow lingered, gently and pervasively, in that small glass-and-plastic stable at Gate 67.

Ray Jenkins

Walk in love, as Christ also hath loved us.

Ephesians 5:2

Keeping CHRISTMAS

Ah dearest Jesus, Holy Child,
Make Thee a bed, soft, undefiled,
Within my heart, that it may be
A quiet chamber kept for Thee.

Martin Luther

FROM LET US KEEP CHRISTMAS

Whatever else be lost among the years,
Let us keep Christmas still a shining thing:
Whatever doubts assail us, or what fears,
Let us hold close one day, remembering
Its poignant meaning for the hearts of men.
Let us get back our childlike faith again.

Grace Noll Crowell

THE BLESSING OF THE CRECHE

One Christmas I traveled to Bethlehem. There is a little shop
there that sits on a winding road, not far from the nativity cave.
As I stepped inside, a dark-eyed man with a wide, white smile
appeared at my elbow. "May I help you, Madam?" he said.

"I'm looking for a creche," I replied. "A nativity set."

His eyes gleamed like two black pearls. He made a little bow
to the rear of the store. I followed him along an aisle until suddenly he stepped aside, sweeping out his arm, and there in the
middle of a table sat a creche. A creche so splendid it seemed
to glow with the ancient holiness that inspired it. It had been
carved from the olive trees that dotted the Judean hills like green
umbrellas. The rich wood shone warm and golden in the dim
light of the little shop. I touched each piece with reverence. Only
moments before I had stood in the heart of the holy cave where
Jesus was born and my heart was still full.

The salesman stood nearby. "You like, Madam?" he asked,
as my fingers touched the tiny tips of the star carved atop the
stable.

He stepped closer. "It is the finest wood. And the workman-
ship is unmatched," he said. I nodded.

I walked around the table, trying to make up my mind. "I'm
not sure," I said.

"Ah, but Madam, you must have it!" he said. "A Bethlehem
creche has secret blessings!"

In the end I purchased the creche, not for its alleged "secret

blessings," but because of its irresistible beauty and because I was in Bethlehem and the long-ago miracle still lived in the air.

I stored it in a cardboard box in the attic. The next Christmas, I wanted to make the creche's first appearance beneath our tree special. I thought and wondered. How could it touch my family with the Bethlehem miracle? I found myself remembering the words of the salesman, "A Bethlehem creche has secret blessings." Perhaps he was right. Perhaps God *could* bless and inspire our lives through its presence, if only we let Him. And not just with a Bethlehem creche…but *any* creche, even the tiny one my daughter had made from popsicle sticks one Christmas past.

So I sat down and wrote a prayer. Then, filled with anticipation, I climbed to the attic and brought down the cardboard box. That night, with the tree lights shining in the darkness and dancing on the windows, my family gathered around the tree. An almost reverent silence settled about us as softly as a whisper in church. My husband opened the lid. The children took turns standing each item of the creche beneath the tree as I read my prayer aloud:

It is time, Lord. Time to take the holy drama from this cardboard box and set it beneath the tree. As I blow away the dust, may this little creche come to life in our home and bestow its secret blessings.

Bless this wooden stable, Lord. This lowly abode of cows and donkeys. May it keep me humble this Christmas.

Bless this tiny star beaming at the top. May it light my eyes with the wonder of Your caring.

Bless the little angel. May her song flow through our house and fill it with smiles.

Bless this caring shepherd and the small lamb cradled in his arms. May it whisper of Your caring embrace on my life.

Bless these Wise Men bearing splendid gifts. May they inspire me to lay my shining best at Your feet.

Bless this earthly father in his simple robe. May he remind me of all You have entrusted to my care.

Bless this Virgin Mother. May she teach me patience as I tend to my own little ones.

And bless this Baby nestled in the hay. May the love He brought to earth that Bethlehem night so fill my heart with compassion and warmth that it becomes a Christmas gift to those around me.

Now the creche is here, Lord…and we are holy participants in Your miracle night.

May Your secret blessings come to us as a spark from Your glory…a candle that never goes out.

Amen

I can't tell you *exactly* what happened to us that night, but I do know that I experienced a special holiness and a reverence for our family that stayed with me all through the Christmas season. That was my "secret blessing," and perhaps each of us shared the same "secret." For this little ritual has become the single most important Christmas preparation for our family.

Sue Monk Kidd

Long, Long Ago

Winds through the olive trees
Softly did blow,
Round little Bethlehem
Long, long ago.

Sheep on the hillside lay
Whiter than snow;
Shepherds were watching them
Long, long ago.

Then from the happy sky
Angels bent low,
Singing their songs of joy
Long, long ago.

For in a manger bed,
Cradled we know,
Christ came to Bethlehem
Long, long ago.

Author Unknown

For God so loved the world,
that he gave his only begotten
Son, that whosoever believeth
in him should not perish, but
have everlasting life.

John 3:16

And it came to pass in those days, that there went out a decree from Caesar Augustus, that all the world should be taxed…

And all went to be taxed, every one into his own city.

And Joseph also went up from Galilee, out of the city of Nazareth, into Judaea, unto the city of David, which is called Bethlehem; (because he was of the house and lineage of David:)

To be taxed with Mary his espoused wife, being great with child.

And so it was, that, while they were there, the days were accomplished that she should be delivered.

And she brought forth her firstborn son, and wrapped him in swaddling clothes, and laid him in a manger; because there was no room for them in the inn.

And there were in the same country shepherds abiding in the field, keeping watch over their flock by night.

And, lo, the angel of the Lord came upon them, and the glory of the Lord shone round about them: and they were sore afraid.

And the angel said unto them, Fear not: for, behold, I bring you good tidings of great joy, which shall be to all people.

For unto you is born this day in the city of David a Saviour, which is Christ the Lord.

And this shall be a sign unto you; Ye shall find the babe wrapped in swaddling clothes, lying in a manger.

And suddenly there was with the angel a multitude of the heavenly host praising God, and saying,

Glory to God in the highest, and on earth peace, good will toward men.

Luke 2:1, 3–14

THE FIRST CHRISTMAS

Remember in the busy moments of the Christmas days—what it really means. Then lift your heart in prayer and praise—to the God who gave His son to show the world The Way. Think of this; remembering the first glad Christmas Day.

In a small Judean town unto a Jewish maid—a child was born. In stable straw the little One was laid—because the inn was crowded and no room was there for them. But history was made that night in tiny Bethlehem.

The Christmas era had commenced: a truth to set men free— had come as light in darkness to redeem humanity…No wonder that an angel throng proclaimed that infant's birth—heralding the Saviour and Redeemer of the earth.

Patience Strong

Angels, from the realms of glory,
Wing your flight o'er all the earth;
Ye, who sang creation's story,
Now proclaim Messiah's birth:
Come and worship, come and worship,
Worship Christ, the newborn King.

James Montgomery

MY CHRISTMAS PRAYER

Dearest God, please never let me
Crowd my life full to the brim.
So like the keeper of Bethlehem's inn,
I find I have no room for Him.

Instead, let my heart's door be ever open,
Ready to welcome the newborn King,
Let me offer the best I have,
To Him who gives me everything.

Rosalyn Hart Finch

71

THE CHRISTMAS IN MAMA'S KITCHEN

For years, we put the Christmas tree in the parlor. It was the fanciest room in the old farmhouse—carpeted, wallpapered and curtained. It seemed fitting to celebrate the Master's birthday in the best room.

However, there was too much activity going on from day to day in the big kitchen—Mama's kitchen—to maintain an unused fire elsewhere, so there wasn't always a fire burning in the parlor. Grandma and Mama cooked, sewed, churned, washed and ironed in the kitchen. Dad and Grandpa kept their accounts, read the papers, soled shoes there. My two sisters and I did homework, helped with the chores, played our games there. Mama's kitchen fireplace was always aglow, the range constantly fired. It was a big spacious room—bright and cozy.

On December Sundays or special holidays, when company was expected, Dad would make a fire in the parlor stove and we'd all go in to enjoy the tree, breathe its cedary fragrance, touch the old familiar baubles. Baby Jesus, in his crib in the creche beneath the tree, would, after a long time, feel warm to our touch.

But somehow the parlor never had the coziness Mama's kitchen had. I always liked the big center table we gathered around, face to face, making small talk or sometimes serious talk. If Mama read a Christmas story aloud in the parlor, it wasn't the same as in the kitchen accompanied by the sputtering fireplace and singing teakettle. Even our evening prayers seemed to come naturally in the kitchen.

One winter evening, as the fire died in the parlor stove, I boldly lifted the crib from the creche and took it into the kitchen, setting it near the fireplace. My sisters, thinking I had been irreverent, told Mama.

"Let it be," Mama said. She smiled at me, though I had expected a reprimand.

The next Christmas, when Dad and Grandpa brought the tree home, Mama said, "I mean to put it up here in the kitchen this year."

Celebrate His birthday in here with the smell of cabbage cooking, the butter being churned, our old barn clothes hanging over there?" one of my sisters demanded.

"Let's try it," Mama said.

The hatrack was moved a little closer to the sewing machine. The cot was pushed up against another wall to make room. When we came downstairs for breakfast, in from the outdoor chores, home from school, there was the tree, bright, warm and fragrant. We trimmed it leisurely, cranberry chains one evening, popcorn garlands the next. Baby Jesus, in the crib, close and dear, was always warm, as were the little sheep, donkeys, shepherds and Wise Men.

When we read the Christmas story, starting seven nights before Christmas so each could have his turn at reading it, the event that happened so long ago and far away now seemed so close, as if it might have happened just last night in our own cow stable. I could visualize the Baby lying in Star's haylined feed box; hear the soft, velvety whinny of Dobbin looking on through the bars; the stirrings of other creatures that had come in from the cold.

The moon and stars that the shepherds saw that night in their pastures were the same moon and stars that shone on me when I went to close the chicken house door. White-bearded Grandpa, coming in from the snowy outdoors, bearing a gift of shiny red apples from the apple hole, looked very much like a Wise Man. We didn't know what had happened to our Christmas, but we knew it was better than any we'd ever had.

One afternoon a neighbor dropped in with some cookies. "Why, Myrtle," she said to Mama, "is this—is—this—appropriate—" Her voice trailed off. But after looking around the kitchen her face lit up. "Myrtle," she exclaimed, "you've brought Christmas in here to be an everyday thing, warm and comfortable, right amongst your living!"

Mama smiled and replied, "Only our best for the Master." She may have winked at me. I don't know. Fireplace shadows sometimes play tricks, and holiday eyes get so bright they have to blink often.

Jean Bell Mosley

We hear the Christmas angels
The great glad tidings tell;
O come to us, abide with us,
Our Lord Immanuel!

The door is on the latch tonight,
The hearth-fire is aglow,
I seemed to hear soft passing feet—
The Christ child in the snow.

My heart is open wide tonight
For stranger, kith or kin.
I would not bar a single door
Where Love might enter in.

Kate Douglas Wiggen

GRAMMY'S CRECHE

The Grammy who started it all was my mother, Adela Rogers St. Johns. It was after I moved to California with my two-year-old daughter, Kristen and six-year-old son, George. We all lived together, along with an aunt and uncle and various friends and relations, in a family compound called *The Hill*.

As Christmas approached, Grammy decided more than one Christmas tree was redundant, so for her house she bought, instead, a sturdy, rustic, peak-roofed shed, charming Mary and Joseph figurines, a small wooden manger, and of course the Royal Infant Himself. The whole was set up on a living room table surrounded with holiday greens and poinsettias. (The Infant hidden snugly out of sight until Christmas Eve.) The children thought the very merry Christmas tree at our house was for "pretty"; but at Grammy's house, where we gathered together on Christmas Eve, and Baby Jesus appeared in the manger, Grammy's creche, though simple, was the focus of reverence and awe.

Small wonder that Kristen and George started to save from their pocket money to add to Grammy's creche. On those long-ago Christmas Eves, as we read the Christmas story from the Gospels, the children would present their gifts. One year an exotic Wise Man; another, four tiny shepherds and one too-large sheep; then a blue ceramic donkey, a plump porcelain angel with a rose atop her head…

The children grew up, married and moved away. Grammy's

work as a writer led her to move permanently to a hotel in New York. *The Hill* was no more and the creche went into storage.

Then my granddaughter was born. It was just before Jessica's first Christmas that a large package was delivered to me from the storage warehouse. The card read, "From one grandmother to another." It was Grammy's creche. And there they were—Mary and Joseph and Jesus, the Wise Man, the big sheep and too-small shepherds, the blue donkey minus one ear, the angel *sans* rose, but what matter? I carefully set the scene on a table in the living room. After all, more than one Christmas tree is redundant!

It was before this manger that Jessica and later her brother Bogart learned the blessed Christmas story and the beloved carols. And then these two began to bring gifts to the stable. An early offering was a tiny gift-wrapped package of peanuts. Later, with allowances hoarded throughout December, Christmas by Christmas, arrived a variety of angels, several deer, a cow, and more odd sheep. Not quite every beast of the field nor all the great sea monsters gathered before the Holy Family, but there did appear a white horse, an otter, a lion, a handsome orangu-tan, Jonah's whale and, since Bo found out what Behemoth meant, a hippopotamus.

Grammy's creche became a neighborhood attraction, with all the children dropping by each year during Christmas week to watch it grow.

Two years ago, Jessica and Bo made an Advent wreath to place at the manger site, and each of the four Sundays before Christmas we ceremoniously lighted a candle and sang carols.

This past year they arranged the scene themselves, using my brick fireplace with its raised hearth. Books, stacked to form a series of gentle terraces to the hearth, were covered with a white sheet and cotton snow, sure footing for men and their beasts. The fireplace was filled with pine boughs from their yard, and on the hearth itself was the creche with its familiar, well-loved figures.

On Christmas Eve, as Jessica, now ten, placed the Infant in His manger and her mother, father, Bo and I sang one last "Silent Night," I inwardly thanked my mom for her gift. Not only for the tangible objects themselves but for her gift of wisdom in establishing a tradition that strengthens our family and its sense of continuity. For one day, I know, in the not-too-distant future, I will give my daughter Grammy's creche, "From one grandmother to another."

Elaine St. Johns

KEEPING CHRISTMAS

There is a better thing than the observance of Christmas day and that is keeping Christmas.

Are you willing

to forget what you have done for other people, and

to remember what other people have done for you;

to ignore what the world owes you, and to think what you owe the world;

to put your rights in the background, and your duties in the middle distance, and your chances to do a little more than your duty in the foreground;

to see that your fellow men are just as real as you are, and try to look behind their faces to their hearts, hungry for joy;

to own that probably the only good reason for your existence is not what you are going to get out of life, but what you are going to give;

to close your book of complaints against the management of the universe, and look around you for a place where you can sow a few seeds of happiness—

are you willing to do these things even for a day?

Then you can keep Christmas.

Are you willing to stoop down and consider the needs and the desires of little children;

to remember the weakness and loneliness of people who are growing old;

to stop asking how much your friends love you, and ask yourself whether you love them enough;

to bear in mind the things that other people have to bear in their hearts;

to try to understand what those who live in the same home with you really want, without waiting for them to tell you;

to trim your lamp so that it will give more light and less smoke, and to carry it in front so that your shadow will fall behind you;

to make a grave for your ugly thoughts, and a garden for your good thoughts, with the gate open—

are you willing to do these things even for a day?

Then you can keep Christmas.

Are you willing to believe that love is the strongest thing in the world—stronger than hate, stronger than evil, stronger than death—and that the blessed life which began in Bethlehem nineteen hundred years ago is the image and brightness of the Eternal Love?

Then you can keep Christmas.

And if you keep it for a day, why not always?

But you can never keep it alone.

Henry Van Dyke

IF EVERY DAY WERE CHRISTMAS

If the spirit of Christmas were with us every day, some revolutionary events would occur:

Selfishness would die a death of starvation.

Avarice would be hung higher than Haman.

Foolish pride would go down in crushing defeat.

Senseless strife and silly bickerings would shame each other to death.

The prayer of Jesus for the unity of His followers would be answered.

Racial animosities would be drowned in a sea of brotherhood.

"Peace on earth" would become a glorious reality.

Edgar De Witt Jones

SILENT NIGHT

This year on Christmas Eve my husband John and I will get into our car and drive, as always, to our familiar brightly lit church with its swelling organ and banked poinsettia plants. But this year we'll also be driving, in a sense, to another church, a church on the other side of the world, and we'll be thinking of our new Chinese friend, Dr. Li.

Dr. Li is an elderly physician who studied in the United States during the 1930s, but who lives now in Shanghai. John and I met him there on a Sunday when we'd gone to seek out a Christian church we'd heard about. We found the church somewhere in the middle of that enormous city on a street thronged with bicycles and pedestrians all dressed in dark green Mao jackets and loose-fitting trousers. The building was red brick, with tall Gothic windows, and to our surprise it was filled with worshippers; every pew was packed, people sitting in aisles, on the windowsills, standing around the walls.

"How long has this church been here?" we asked Dr. Li.

"A long time," he replied in flawless English, "but only three months ago did it re-open." Then, through the thick spectacles that he wore, we caught a glimmer of tears. "It opened again on Christmas Eve," he said.

For the first few years after the Communist victory in 1949, he told us, churchgoing, though disapproved of and discouraged, was still possible. But gradually all churches were closed, boarded up or converted to warehouses—this building in the summer of 1959. For months Dr. Li and his wife tried to accustom themselves to life without the punctuation of that weekly Sunday gathering—especially important where Christians were in such a minority.

Christmas Eve, 1959, was chill and drizzly. At the hospital, it was an evening shift like any other. Only in Dr. Li's thoughts, and perhaps, those of the handful of other Christians on the staff, was there the awareness that this was the night when angels sang.

Dr. Li got back to his two-room apartment around ten, but he could not settle down. At eleven he went into the bedroom intending to get undressed. Instead, he whirled suddenly and headed for the front door. Although not a word had been said, his wife followed him into the deserted street. Through the icy drizzle they walked, moving silently so as to attract no attention.

Left at the corner, across a square, right onto the avenue— both knew without saying it that they were headed for the church. There it loomed ahead, dark and padlocked—but solid too, and somehow comforting. *I really am here*, it seemed to say. *I really came to earth this night, not just as a longing, but in a form you can see and touch.*

As they drew still closer they became aware of other silent walkers. From every side street they came, alone and in twos and threes, converging on the avenue. Soon hundreds were standing shoulder to shoulder in the dark churchyard. Newcomers took up their posts on the sidewalks. For over two hours they stood in the rain while Christmas came. No hymns, no sermon. Only *He is born! He is with us!* in unspoken communion around the shuttered church.

For 20 years, Dr. Li told us, this was their Christmas Eve observance. No outward agreement, so far as he knew, was ever made beforehand to do so. Just, on this night, in homes and apartments all over this part of Shanghai, people silently put on their coats and came to stand here together.

And so it is that this Christmas Eve, when John and I arrive at church we won't have to wait for the communion service to begin. With the first impulse that says "Go!"—with the first longing to share this night with others—the real communion, the undefeatable one, will have begun.

Elizabeth Sherrill

Make me pure, Lord; Thou art holy;
Make me meek, Lord; Thou wert lowly;
Now beginning, and alway:
Now begin, on Christmas day.

Gerard Manley Hopkins

DAY OF HOPE

Christmas is the one day of the year that carries real hope and promise for all mankind.

It carries the torch of brotherhood.

It is the one day in the year when most of us grow big of heart and broad of mind.

It is the single day when most of us are as kind and as thoughtful of others as we know how to be;

when most of us are as gracious and generous as we would like always to be;

when the joy of the home is more important than the profits of the office;

when peoples of all races speak cheerfully to each other when they meet;

when high and low wish each other well;

and the one day when even enemies forgive and forget.

Edgar A. Guest

CHRISTMAS BELLS

I heard the bells on Christmas Day
Their old, familiar carols play,
And wild and sweet
The words repeat
Of peace on earth, good-will to men!

Henry Wadsworth Longfellow

ACKNOWLEDGMENTS

The editor and the publisher have made every effort to trace the ownership of all copyrighted material and to secure permission from copyright holders of such material. In the event of any question arising as to the use of any material, the publisher and editor, while expressing regret for inadvertent error, will be pleased to make the necessary corrections in future printings. Thanks are due to the following authors, publishers, publications and agents for permission to use the material indicated.

Christian Herald Association for "If Every Day Were Christmas" by Edgar Dewitt Jones from *Fifty Years of Christmas*, copyright © 1951 by Christian Herald Association; for "Day of Hope" by Edgar Guest from *Fifty Years of Christmas*, copyright © 1951 by Christian Herald Association.

Lois Duncan for "Heavenly Child." (Good Housekeeping, 1972 and 1975). Copyright © 1982 by the Hearst Company.

Friends United Press, Richmond, Indiana and the Howard Thurman Educational Trust for "Gifts on My Altar" by Howard Thurman from *The Mood of Christmas*, 1985.

Guideposts Associates, Inc. for the following selections from *The Gifts of Christmas*, copyright © 1981 by Guideposts Associates, Inc., Carmel, N.Y. 10512: "Snead's Christmas Gift" by James McDermott, "The Blessing of the Creche" by Sue Monk Kidd, "My Christmas Prayer" by Rosalyn Hart Finch, "Silent Night" by Elizabeth Sherrill. For the following selections from *The Guideposts Family Christmas Book*, copyright © 1980 by Guideposts Associates, Inc., Carmel, N.Y. 10512: "The Christmas in Mama's Kitchen" by Jean Bell Mosley, "Grammy's Creche" by Elaine St. Johns. Reprinted by permission.

Harper & Row, Publishers, Inc. for "Let Us Keep Christmas" from *Poems of Inspiration and Courage* by Grace Noll Crowell, copyright © 1950 by Harper & Row, Publishers Inc. Reprinted by permission.

The New York Times Company for an excerpt from "The Quiet Drama at Gate 67, in Atlanta" by Ray Jenkins, December 25, 1979, copyright © 1979 by The New York Times Company, excerpted from "Drama at Gate 67" by Ray Jenkins, Reader's Digest, December 1980. Reprinted by permission.

Harold Ober Associates Incorporated for "Christmas Day In The Morning" by Pearl S. Buck, copyright © 1955 by Pearl S. Buck. Copyright renewed 1983. Reprinted by permission.

The Reader's Digest Assn., Inc. for "The Touch of a Hand" by Mary Janes. Reprinted with permission from the December 1982 *Reader's Digest*. Copyright © 1982 by the Reader's Digest Assn., Inc.; for "A Young Girl's Gift" by Elizabeth Starr Hill. Excerpted with permission from the December 1966 *Reader's Digest*. Copyright © 1966 by The Reader's Digest Assn., Inc.

Fleming H. Revell Company for "When Christmas Came To Bethlehem" by Charles L. Allen and Charles L. Wallis, copyright © 1963 by Fleming H. Revell Company; for "Christmas In

Our Hearts" by Charles L. Allen and Charles L. Wallis, copyright © 1957 by Fleming H. Revell Company. Reprinted by permission.

Rupert Crew Limited for "The Christmas Child" by Patience Strong from her book, *Harbours of Happiness*, published by Muller, Blond & White, by permission of Rupert Crew Limited; for "Messages of Christmas" from *Roses for Remembrance* by Patience Strong, published by Muller, Blond & White, by permission of Rupert Crew Limited; for "The First Christmas" by Patience Strong from her book *Passing Clouds*, published by Muller, Blond & White. Reprinted by permission of Rupert Crew Limited.

Charles Scribner's Sons for "Keeping Christmas" by Henry Van Dyke from *Six Days of the Week*. Copyright © 1924 Charles Scribner's Sons; copyright renewed 1952 Tertius Van Dyke. Reprinted with permission.

Viking Penquin Inc. for "The Maid-Servant at The Inn" from *The Portable Dorothy Parker*, edited by Brendan Gill. Copyright © 1928, renewed 1956 by Dorothy Parker. Reprinted by permission.

Book design by Betsy Beach
Type set in Cheltenham light with italic